INDIVIDUALS, JOURNALISM, AND SOCIETY
EPILOGUE-LESSONS LEARNED

Screenplay by

Stephen B. Waters

Nefarious people have joined in a new
battle for your mind. They believe your
individuality doesn't matter, that
journalism serves them alone, and that
society expects them to rule.

While most schooling leaves people
defenseless against their words, this
synthesis will help defend against their
bold misuse of ideas.

Stephen B. Waters
6391 Karlen Rd.
Rome, NY 13440

sbwaters@rnymedia.com

Waters, Stephen B.
    Individuals, Journalism, and Society—Epilogue/ Stephen B. Waters
    ISBN-13: 978-0-9845258-9-8 (Paperback)
    ISBN-13: 978-0-9845258-8-1 (E-Book)

Published by:
    Stephen Waters
    6391 Karlen Rd.
    Rome, NY 13440

Author's Note

Individuals, Journalism, and Society was begun in November, 2008, and published in 2010. Those three concepts overlay each other like concentric circles. What is important for one is important to the adjacent circles.

Decade by decade IJ&S examined the 20th century to reveal why it failed to live up to expectations. It concludes with what might be done to salvage both culture and society.

This epilogue adds much of what happened since 2010 to pinpoint cultural and societal threats and synthesizes a measured response. Writing in the form of a screenplay makes it more accessible. The form makes it easy to produce short programs for theater, dramatic readings, video for online streaming, or television.

Written originally in Socratic dialogue, IJ&S has also been rewritten in screenplay format as 19 independent episodes that can be produced independently or spread out as lessons over several semesters or seasons.

Incidentally, The name Brad pays homage to my grandfather — artist, athlete, and a wise and principled newspaper publisher. Janet is named after a fictional Brad and Janet couple out of respect for the humor required to sort out what matters in life.

Regards/Stephen

Stephen Waters is the fifth generation of his family to own the Rome (NY) Daily Sentinel, where he worked for 46 years. Earlier he programmed computers for IBM, salvaged a university computer center in Nijmegen, The Netherlands, majored in History and Political Science at Colgate University, and spent a year as a high school exchange student in Australia.

INDIVIDUALS, JOURNALISM, AND SOCIETY

<u>EPISODE 20 - EPILOGUE-LESSONS LEARNED</u>

INT. BEDROOM - MORNING

Twelve years have passed since publisher Brad's chronology of Election Day, 2008, hour by hour, recording lessons learned.

Brad opens bedroom curtains as his teacher wife rests in bed.

>   BRAD
> "Morning, sweetheart!"

>   JANET
> Morning, dear. What's up?"

>   BRAD
> Looking over the lake again. — It's been twelve years since I wrote "Individuals, Journalism, and Society." I'd like to say much is the same but it's different.

>   JANET
> Well, you're older, ache more, have retired from the newspaper, and keep busy with your grandson.

>   BRAD
> So many people still can't see the lessons learned.

>   JANET
> Like what?

INT. BEDROOM - MOMENTS LATER

First lesson: Who owns society?

>   BRAD
> Like whose society is this?

>   JANET
> Which society?

>   BRAD
> Our immediate society, but it applies generally. Who owns it? You or me?

>   JANET
> We do individually and together. There is no ruler.

                    BRAD
          What if I assume I'm in charge and start
          setting new rules.

                    JANET
          There will be Hell to pay. And I won't
          leave; I'll send you packing.

                    BRAD
          Why don't others stand up for that in the
          larger society? — Come on out on the
          porch. I just made fresh coffee.

                    JANET
          Great!

INT. PORCH - MOMENTS LATER

Second lesson: Resolving differences.

As they move to the porch overlooking the lake, they talk,
pour coffee, and sit down.

                    BRAD
          Second lesson: In society, then, how
          should people resolve differences?

                    JANET
          Tacitly agree to work under an umbrella
          of peaceful problem resolution — a
          process built on trust that justice is
          applied without favor.

                    BRAD
          Suppose I pack the court, restrict what
          you can say, or count the ballots myself?

                    JANET
          Then you play a risky game with no
          guarantee you will win.

                    BRAD
          Yes, it could get nasty so, instead, let
          me try to bluff you: Accuse you of having
          taken advantage of me for years, redefine
          words to flummox you. ... Cheat.

                    JANET
          I don't like where this is headed.

INT. PORCH - MOMENTS LATER

Third lesson: Which is the greater political risk?

                    BRAD
So, for 1) society belongs to
individuals, not the self-chosen few and,
2) anyone fiddling with problem
resolution risks everything. ... But
there is a third lesson that underscores
the previous two: Is your greater fear
the angst that politicians conjure up
during an emergency or the danger that
under the guise of that emergency they
might grasp for permanent control?

                    JANET
Good question. Definitely their grab for
control. The first damages the surface
level of cultures and people, but the
latter rips the underlying fabric of
society that ties all individuals
together.

                    BRAD
Exactly. People seldom see that culture
and society are different. Cultures are
like the varied and different pile of a
carpet. Society is the warp and weft
thread underneath that holds the pile of
the carpet together.

                    JANET
People also seldom see that society forms
at an edge where any two individuals or
cultures meet and where, by their
actions, they buy in to the humility and
reciprocity that are the minimum
requirements for society.

                    BRAD
Civilizations are tissue thin. They can
collapse in less than a single
generation. Those who seek power without
humility and reciprocity tend to misuse
that control in ways that quickly drag
others back down to the Law of the Jungle
that took so long to climb out of.

                    JANET
People struggled for thousands of years
to lift themselves a tiny fraction above
an animal world that had no morality, and
these bastards would destroy it because
their personalities won't let them face
themselves in a mirror.

                    BRAD
          Just as parasites co-opt a host, they'll
          hijack a political base. Their latest
          game used postmodernism to hijack
          liberalism after which they abandoned
          everything for which it stood. Classical
          liberalism was open-minded, believed in
          individualism, and applied human values
          universally.

                    JANET
          Fools and charlatans on both sides use
          postmodernism so this isn't about
          Republicans or Democrats. Some with
          warped thinking are shallow, others mean,
          but the more dangerous are those who
          built their morality at odds with
          reality.

INT. PORCH - MOMENTS LATER

Fourth lesson: People think differently and not always
clearly.

                    BRAD
          When personal experience shows their
          beliefs are at odds with what is real,
          they assume reality must be changed
          instead of their beliefs. They pick and
          choose what "science" is to reinforce
          their preconceived notions.

                    JANET
          Schools mostly overlook that rationality
          isn't how we think but rather, once a
          conclusion is reached, how we check our
          work. Sperry and Gazzaniga earned a Nobel
          Prize in 1968 that showed that many
          conclusions well up from beneath one's
          consciousness.

                    BRAD
          The fourth lesson is that people often
          think they are right, not because they
          are right, but just because they *think*
          they are right. — Some not only don't
          want to check their work, their egos
          won't let them check their work.

                    JANET
          That creates problems for those obliged
          to deal with them.

> BRAD
> Therapy can sometimes help, but often
> those with a distorted view of reality
> don't recognize they need help.

> JANET
> When people like that gather in groups
> they reinforce defective logic inside the
> group and out, leading to pseudo-reality,
> and pseudo-morality.

> BRAD
> The larger the group, the more they bully
> the community to conform to their warped
> perceptions. It's as if *Clockwork Orange*
> merged with *Bonfire of the Vanities*.
> Imagine an anti-social delinquent like
> Alex joined with the 1500s Friar
> Savonarola to give you villainy that
> can't face itself. Alex bullied and
> Savonarola savaged history and mirrors.

INT. PORCH - MOMENTS LATER

Fifth lesson: Groupthink often fosters distorted ideas,
realities, and moralities.

> JANET
> Most people don't expect aberrant
> malevolence in others. Most trust others
> to use logic like their own, test
> conclusions, and use consistent morality.
> It's reasonable to expect others to be
> reasonable even when they disagree with
> you, to expect they will respectfully
> challenge ideas but not lash out
> personally — even if their talk and
> action reveal conflicts with reality.

> BRAD
> Once in power they push their fantasy.
> They bully more — ostracize, shun,
> punish, and economically cripple those
> with whom they disagree. They treat
> objection as criminal and, whatever isn't
> yet a crime, their double standards treat
> as one.

> JANET
> Ancient Greeks would say their logic
> subverts *logos* and their morality
> dominates *ethos*.

BRAD
They won't admit Postmodernism's logical
inconsistency consumed itself after the
1950s. It should have died in 1872 when
Lewis Carroll skewered its slipperiness
in *Through the Looking Glass*.

JANET
Yes, Humpty Dumpty had the audacity to
claim, "When I use a word it means just
what I choose it to mean — neither more
nor less." That's when Alice challenged
him, "The question is whether you can
make words mean so many different
things."

BRAD
Carroll's readers laughed when Dumpty
falsely claimed authority, "The question
is which is to be master — that's all."
Yet, since the 1960s, postmodernism
jumped out of philosophy and literature
like a virus jumps species, to infect
politicians, educationists, community
organizers, pontificators and
journalists.

JANET
Postmodernism always struggles after
power. It squabbles over interpretations,
pushing this narrative over that, but
their myths are dishonest and incomplete.

BRAD
Then the fifth lesson is that
postmodernists don't bother to validate
their claims because, by definition, they
are valid simply because they are theirs.
Meanwhile, they discard any claim of
yours because it is not theirs. They
don't find that at all inconsistent.

JANET
They insist you change your mind because
they say so.

BRAD
Machiavelli would admire that they
undermine every peaceful process of
conflict resolution and return to the Law
of the Jungle.

                    JANET
          If an ethical framework one advocates
          doesn't value honesty there is nothing in
          it for anyone. You can't contrive a story
          that ends up less reasonable than what
          you criticize.

                    BRAD
          Absurdly, many of today's institutions
          buy into the fraud just as Antonio
          Gramsci predicted. While war would not
          defeat western culture, it can fall to a
          long march through its institutions.
          Gramsci's scheme feeds the defective
          logic that reality should bend to their
          fantasy. If they don't impose their
          pseudo-reality on the rest of us, they
          would have to face that they're the ones
          who don't measure up.

                    JANET
          You claim that, but can you prove it?

                    BRAD
          Easily. Look at how they turn away all
          objections rather than address them. They
          dissemble, even to themselves. Focus on
          what they say and do and their fractures
          become obvious. Ultimately, they claim to
          stand for all that is "good" in society
          but, because they see society as theirs
          to control, they don't believe in society
          at all.

INT. PORCH - MOMENTS LATER

Sixth lesson: People suffering distorted reality gull other
people.

                    JANET
          With single individuals, such
          psychological problems are more easily
          detected and therapy can be offered.

                    BRAD
          But gathered into self-reinforcing
          groups, they acquire increasing social
          influence to pressure others to conform,
          believe, and pretend.

                    JANET
          You can see it so many places: In
          Hollywood they compliment bad acting with
          air-kisses, in academia they bestow

lifetime courtesy titles for sometimes
trivial theses, in politics they offer an
obsequious title "honorable gentleman or
gentle lady" for those who are anything
but.

                BRAD
The sixth lesson is that such intertwined
pseudo-authorities depreciate word
meanings and analytic skills to entice
you to look through their lens of
artificial reality.

                JANET
You'd think that would be isolated.

                BRAD
Why? Pseudo-journalists pander for
political access. Pseudo-politicians
pander to corporate contributors. Pseudo-
teachers pander to bureaucracy. Pseudo-
community organizers, inveigle themselves
into influence peddling, claiming
"rights" as stakeholders. Pseudo-
businessmen pander to public regulators.
And they all pander to mold new
generations of panderers.

                JANET
That leaves us adrift in a sea of
uncertainty with no one else to trust.
What can one do?

                BRAD
Figure out who deserves trust.

INT. PORCH - MOMENTS LATER

Action #1: Mistrust those who claim expertise.

                JANET
People are reluctant to check the work of
those who govern them. They cede checks
and balances to those who simply claim
authority with little integrity and a
worse track record.

                BRAD
Those in power urge us to trust experts,
pushing credentials instead of
understanding. If we don't identify their
past failures, we'll never get real
experts.

                    JANET
          Face it, a real expert is someone who can
          explain things so clearly even we can
          understand.

INT. BEDROOM - MOMENTS LATER

Action #2: Defend against disordered words.

                    BRAD
          You have to defend against words, but so
          many aren't equipped to digest claims
          alleged experts might make.

                    JANET
          People seldom concede when others
          exercise better judgment than their own.

                    BRAD
          Ancient Rome didn't, leading to its
          collapse around 500 A.D. Not until 300
          years later around 800 AD, did
          Charlemagne institute schooling to
          correct weak thinking that too easily
          could undermine a culture.

                    JANET
          His schools sought to teach people to
          think clearly first and only later, in
          graduate classes, to master subjects. He
          decreed that king and commoner would
          study the *Trivium* to validate conclusions
          before they were accepted.

                    BRAD
          That progress was undermined again some
          700 years later, around 1500, when
          educationists eviscerated Charlemagne's
          schooling. They stripped Aristotlean
          rhetoric of its requirement to organize
          and validate what was said.

                    JANET
          They stopped teaching students to defend
          themselves against words, words, words.
          They foolishly started teaching subjects
          hoping students would learn to think.
          There is a difference between "teaching a
          book" and using a book to provoke
          thought.

                    BRAD
          Absent the need to order and validate
          what was said, politics and law became
          shoddy game of salesmanship. Neither

judges nor voters learned enough to care.
We haven't learned a thing! Schools today
teach that Ancient Rome collapsed, but
ignore that long-term tolerance of bad
thought happened more than once and worse
behavior might easily cause it to happen
again.

                    JANET
I'm embarrassed to say that educated
citizens in the early Middle Ages were
better equipped to detect mendacity than
citizens many schools produce today.

                    BRAD
History today is so shallow that citizens
don't know or care that the ancients knew
better! Ancient Greeks called such
overweening pride — hubris.

                    JANET
Ignore history and you may not know until
too late that collapse is imminent. It is
sad to see social, educational, and
political ignorance jeopardize yet
another culture of decent people.

INT. PORCH - MOMENTS LATER

Action #3: Reclaim control of hermeneutics.

                    BRAD
The current war is being fought between
the ears, but who notices? Do you get to
decide the meaning and intent of words
you use to think and converse?
Hermeneutics is the study of who gets to
interpret things. Postmodern activists
want control. Don't give it to them! They
want to privilege their intentions over
yours. They expect you to give up without
a fight.

                    JANET
They assault you at every turn —
politics, news, schools, entertainment,
social media, and on the street — with
every weapon: projection, hate speech,
and cancel culture; false claims of
instigation, dog whistles, and secret
signs; community guidelines, business
vigilantes, and fascist firings for
crime-think; corporate social agendas,
boycotts, book-burning, statue-tipping,

false flags, and physical mobs. It's
pointless for them to impose "Wokeness"
on the past. Those who would control your
thoughts feel their thoughts are
privileged and perfect compared to yours.

> BRAD
> Speech police want to control language to
> kill individuality and replace it with
> linguistic collectivism.

> JANET
> That's revolting.

> BRAD
> Correct. It's attempted revolution.

> JANET
> Real individuality isn't selfish. It's
> humble enough to value community with
> others.

INT. PORCH - MOMENTS LATER

Action #4: Demand the Law of Non-conformity be followed.

> BRAD
> Next, hold activists to their own
> standards. Demand consistency in what
> they say and do. They can't do it.

> JANET
> Aristotle's "Law of non-conformity" says
> a cat cannot be a non-cat. There have no
> consistency in their conclusions. There
> are so many words that describe them —
> unsound, defective, incomplete, childish,
> ... a problem for everyone.

> BRAD
> The examples are endless. 1) They
> advocate tolerance imposed by repression.
> 2) They call for acceptance, compassion,
> empathy, and fairness that is conditional
> and selectively applied. 3) They support
> merit except for special classes of
> people. 5) They stand up for free speech,
> but only for approved subjects. 6) They
> want compromise but only toward their
> goals. — And it is all to support a
> contrived reality that never matches what
> is real.

JANET

1) They never allow their linguistic
games to be checked for consistency or
completeness. 2) They talk past
questions, never stating strong
opposition arguments and never addressing
them. 3) Their arguments are
inconsequential and illogical. 4) Their
word meanings are slippery and vague. 5)
Their premises are unsound, supported by
unworthy warrants. 6) And even if their
premises were valid, they would not lead
to sound conclusions.

BRAD

Want examples of their cognitive
dissonance? 1) The CDC says the flu virus
is down because people wear masks but the
COVID-19 virus is up because people don't
wear masks.

JANET

2) The government wants to test
passengers who fly across the border but
not those who walk across.

BRAD

3) Recycling matters but lifecycle costs
for supposedly renewable power don't
include recycling.

JANET

4) In the name of clean air they reject
oil pipelines for truck and rail
alternatives that increase pollution or
don't work when needed. They act as if
oil bought abroad pollutes less than oil
produced here.

BRAD

5) Governments over-regulate our
productive economy throttling production
they need to pay for their overreach.

JANET

6) Science became consensus that forbids
evidence that might undermine consensus,
turning it into an oracle rather than a
method for asking questions.

BRAD

7) Higher minimum wage kills entry-level
jobs they claim to want people to have.

>   JANET
> 8) You can't defend property because they
> have decided others need it more.

>   BRAD
> 9) Voter ID disenfranchises minorities
> rather than protects their vote, too.

>   JANET
> 10) Others have to pay for what they
> claim is a free lunch.

INT. PORCH - MOMENTS LATER

Action #5: Trust actions, not words.

>   BRAD
> In a sea of warped political accusations,
> dismiss those who have blown smoke or
> tolerated others who did. First and
> foremost, that means so-called
> journalists.

>   JANET
> Many journalists are simply newsreaders
> and cable bookers who take no pride in
> accuracy and, instead, seek validation
> from popularity, access, fees, bogus
> awards, and airtime.

>   BRAD
> Where are pithy questions, analysis of
> feeble rhetoric, or comparisons with past
> promises? We can't shift responsibility
> for understanding the world to the
> national press. They are determined to
> mold you to their views. We pay them but
> they stopped working for us. Perhaps they
> once did under local ownership. Back then
> at least they admitted they wrote from a
> point of view. But now too many seem
> ignorant, compromised, or in cahoots.

>   JANET
> They certainly don't expose, label, and
> laugh at gaslighting, poor rhetoric, and
> silly policy. They push it on you
> unchallenged!

>   BRAD
> Fire them! Now! At the national level
> they never have been journalists. Laugh
> at them. Make them squirm. Pseudo-
> politicians spout gaslight and gibberish.
> Pseudo-journalists repeat it.

Educationists teach it. The opposition
ignores it. And most citizens never
learned to recognize, label, and laugh at
it.

INT. PORCH - MOMENTS LATER

Action #6: Laugh at their inconsistency.

                    JANET
          Is laughter enough?

                    BRAD
          Laughter dissolves the non-reasoning they
          use. Anything stronger than laughter they
          label as subversive and an excuse to
          apply greater force. Defectively powerful
          people will use any reason to clamp down.
          They don't need real reasons to avoid
          wrestling with their pseudo-reality.

                    JANET
          They don't believe in civil society do
          they?

                    BRAD
          They never did. Some individuals across
          history have been builders but others are
          destroyers.

                    JANET
          You see it in how they undermine
          individual freedom, suppress opposition,
          and undermine longstanding useful
          institutions.

                    BRAD
          Label amoral defectives for who they are.

                    JANET
          That's brutal.

                    BRAD
          But accurate when they don't give a shit.
          They prey on those who are naive enough
          to expect others to operate under a moral
          umbrella similar to their own.

                    JANET
          What do such people hope to gain?

                    BRAD
          Underneath all their words, it's how they
          defend themselves from themselves. They
          fear mirrors as much as Dracula did. They

destroy those who challenge their pseudo-reality. Their ego depends on seeing their own mental map of reality as more perfect than reality itself. Power is how they keep real reality distant. They may claim it's just politics. It's not. Real politics doesn't dupe people. Real politics is about encouraging people to come to understanding.

          JANET
Then when people call it a political conflict with socialism or fascism, they miss the mark.

          BRAD
Those are two different concepts with one bad and the other worse. In one case, socialism offers no means to self cleanse because any competition occurs behind the veil. No one guards the guardians. Besides, central planners can't know enough or react fast enough to solve more problems than they create.

          JANET
So the jargon of Political Science obscures the underlying problem of misrepresenting reality and morality.

          BRAD
You can't defeat those strung out on pseudo-reality with logic because they don't see anything to concede. Their slippery language allows them to avoid admitting anything. What crime? In their mind, the only crime is admitting to a crime.

          JANET
That would be sad if it weren't dangerous.

INT. PORCH - MOMENTS LATER

Insight #1: The real battle is to suppress individuality.

          JANET
So the big battle is between individualism and collectivism?

          BRAD
Not really. Focus tighter than that. The fight between socialism or fascism and

capitalism is really a skirmish beneath
the real conflict.

          JANET
The big battle is between ...

          BRAD
Individuals.

          JANET
Individuals against individuals — not
conflicting concepts of government?

          BRAD
While socialism and fascism restrict
individuality in society, they are not as
dangerous as disturbed people who covet
power to control you.

          JANET
What do you mean?

          BRAD
Face the two problems: First, their
twisted logic shows they are unwilling to
see how solutions they propose cause more
problems than they solve. ... And,
second, they don't check their work. They
just don't.

          JANET
When they leave out facts that undermine
their thesis nothing is left but fiction.
They claim to stand for all that is "good
in society" but forcing fiction on others
shows they don't believe in society at
all.

          BRAD
They push away evidence that they don't
measure up. They push it so far into the
future they hope they'll die before they
must face it. They posture that their
words are authoritative and the only
words that matter. They don't validate
their claims. And if challenged, you are
subversive, racist, or guilty of some
other unprovable accusation.

INT. PORCH - MOMENTS LATER

Insight #2: Individuality exposes identity politics as fraud.

JANET

Individual versus individual makes sense, but is identifying it as lust for power enough? Is unwillingness to face reality so strong it compels them to destroy institutions with nothing to replace them?

BRAD

They claim to want a more equitable society but discount merit as an unbiased measure. Entitlement underlies their theme instead of responsibility. They feel entitled to something for nothing. They shoulder no responsibility for family, community, economic growth, and quash every opportunity for progress.

JANET

They created "Intersectionality" to marshal multiple potential forms of discrimination — racism, sexism, and classism — to tear down society - with nothing to replace it.

BRAD

In the end, their followers put their life on the line for a theory that doesn't care about them. Those who claim offense and who have the rings of power would as easily cancel them from society, too. Worse, their belief system crushed by a false claim of liberation gives totalitarianism the opportunity to take hold.

JANET

How far we have descended! A hundred years ago the march of progress was celebrated as the cornerstone of modernism.

BRAD

The trajectory across premodern, modern, and postmodern views of the world tells the story.

JANET

Pre-modernists, before the 17th century believed faith and reason together offered a symbiotic view of the world.

                    BRAD
Then Descartes' Modern view rejected
faith but still believed in progress.
That view collapsed when World Wars I and
II forced people to consider reason can
create havoc on the earth.

                    JANET
Seeing nothing left to anchor their world
view, Leftists turned postmodern. Sadly,
postmodernism offered no brake on
oppressive power.

                    BRAD
Relativism's poison destroyed the final
threads of a shared universe, offering
progress no future. None.

                    JANET
Such deconstruction is a foolish, self-
defeating worldview waiting to implode.
Attacking logic and rationality is what
you do if your ideology has nothing to
offer.

                    BRAD
That hasn't stopped its embrace by many
of today's universities. They would laugh
it down if they saw that when you hold to
a falsehood, you imprison yourself.
Instead they flatten out all objections
until they become meaningless. Their
anti-science isn't science. They forgot
Karl Popper's observation that rather
than prove what's true, science prunes
away what is demonstrably false.

                    JANET
They built a house of forced group
identity to shelter from the storm but it
casts individual followers into the
middle of the storm.

                    BRAD
Identity politics allows no
reconciliation. No counterfactuals are
accepted.

                    JANET
For them, racism is okay if they identify
as something else. They suppress that
assigning classes according to a physical
characteristic is the definition of
racism!

>   BRAD
> Critical Race Theory's circular reasoning
> invariably rejects evidence that
> conflicts with its assertions. Without
> "systemic racism" that creates "white
> privilege" followers can't find "racial
> oppression" needed to justify their
> existence.

>   JANET
> Their claimed racism demands neo-racist
> solutions that further exacerbate racist
> problems.

>   BRAD
> For author Dr. James Lindsay, the flawed
> logic they use does not pursue truth but
> holds on to social grievances. He
> suggests a sensible response for
> reasonable people might be to become
> "super-antiracist" that he defines as
> reasonably colorblind without denying
> real racism when it occurs, treating
> every person as an individual, not a
> member of a racial category, and opposing
> all forms of racism, including Woke neo-
> racism.

>   JANET
> Martin Luther King would have been super-
> antiracist, but CRT progressives minimize
> King's accomplishments.

>   BRAD
> Many universities and institutions don't
> simply embrace the fog that has
> descended; they celebrate it! That leaves
> each individual alone to disperse it.

>   JANET
> Individuals need to learn enough about
> self-refuting positions to defend their
> humanity.

INT. PORCH - MOMENTS LATER

Insight 3: Laugh now, before it's too late.

>   BRAD
> Laugh at them. Make fun of their
> conflicted claims of superior knowledge.
> Make them squirm. They are charlatans,
> not politicians, academics, journalists,
> or activists.

                    JANET
Both common sense and comedy are in short
supply. If enough people laugh, whatever
legitimacy they try to claim will
collapse.

                    BRAD
Better laugh now, even though they may
pursue you in anger. Laugh now, because
if you don't, they will get stronger and
hurt you more. They will hound you, your
family, your business. They will pursue
you until you give up your humanity and
your individuality.

                    JANET
It all comes from lying - to others and
to ourselves. Fydor Dostoevsky said, "A
man who lies to himself, and believes his
own lies, becomes unable to recognize
truth, either in himself or anyone else,
and he ends up losing respect for himself
and for others."

                    BRAD
It's not about authority. It's about you.
Measure your place in your world. I'll
match your quote with Natan Sharansky's
measure of liberation: "In the democratic
society in which you live, can you
express your individual views loudly, in
public and in private, on social media
and at rallies, without fear of being
shamed, excommunicated, or cancelled? ...
Each of us individually decides whether
we want to submit to the crippling
indignity of doublethink, or break the
chains that keep us from expressing our
own thoughts, and becoming whole."

                    JANET
To avoid a dystopian world, resolve to be
individual.

                    BRAD
Yes. There is a way back to civil
society. Tom Wolfe wrote about it in *The
Electric Kool-aid Acid Test* when both
activists and officials pushed Ken Kesey
to take one side or another about war. He
refused to play the game. He took out his
harmonica and played. He made the
powerful uncomfortable. They couldn't

cope. Laughter called regular people back
from political absurdity.

                JANET
On all sides, if the ethical framework
you advocate doesn't value honesty, there
is nothing in it for me.

                BRAD
When you synthesize all that is
happening, who checks consistency and who
does not? Who masters enough rhetoric to
tell the difference? Who resolves that
there is some shit I will not eat? Who
can carefully, cautiously, and with
humor, back away from the precipice?

                JANET
          (Smiling.)
We do — when we make our own choice. Do I
laugh now?

                               FADE OUT:

          END OF EPISODE 20.

Other books by Stephen B. Waters

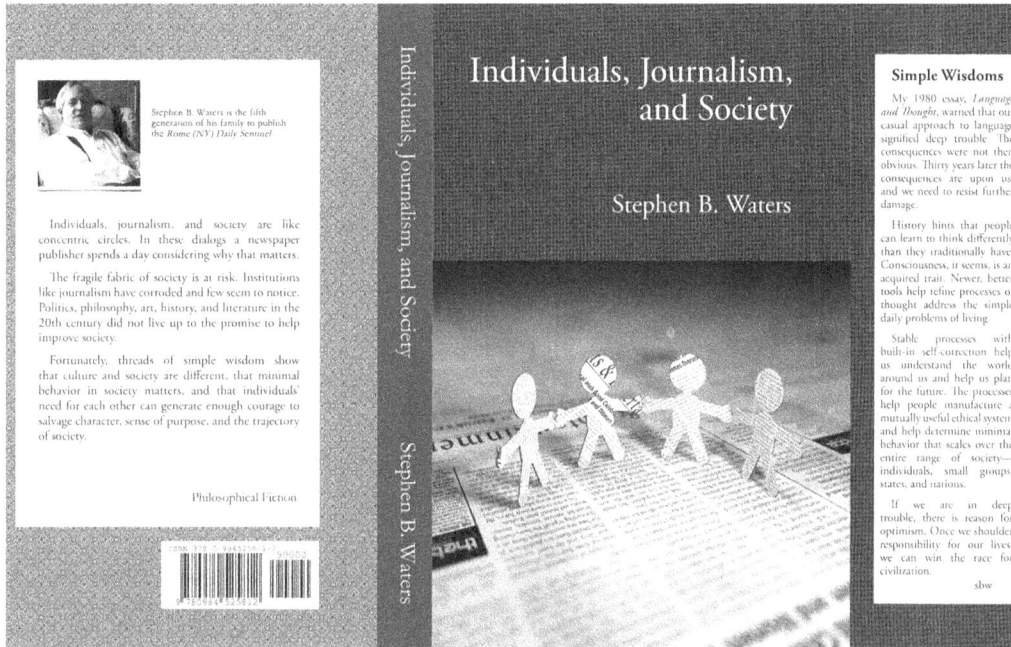

On cover (back): Stephen B. Waters is the fifth generation of his family to publish the Rome (NY) Daily Sentinel

Individuals, journalism, and society are like concentric circles. In these dialogs a newspaper publisher spends a day considering why that matters.

The fragile fabric of society is at risk. Institutions like journalism have corroded and few seem to notice. Politics, philosophy, art, history, and literature in the 20th century did not live up to the promise to help improve society.

Fortunately, threads of simple wisdom show that culture and society are different, that minimal behavior in society matters, and that individuals' need for each other can generate enough courage to salvage character, sense of purpose, and the trajectory of society.

Philosophical Fiction

(spine): Individuals, Journalism, and Society   Stephen B. Waters

(front cover): Individuals, Journalism, and Society

Stephen B. Waters

Simple Wisdoms

My 1980 essay, *Language and Thought*, warned that our casual approach to language signified deep trouble. The consequences were not then obvious. Thirty years later the consequences are upon us, and we need to resist further damage.

History hints that people can learn to think differently than they traditionally have. Consciousness, it seems, is an acquired trait. Newer, better tools help refine processes of thought address the simple daily problems of living.

Stable processes with built-in self-correction help us understand the world around us and help us plan for the future. The processes help people manufacture a mutually useful ethical system and help determine minimal behavior that scales over the entire range of society—individuals, small groups, states, and nations.

If we are in deep trouble, there is reason for optimism. Once we shoulder responsibility for our lives, we can win the race for civilization.

sbw

Individuals, Journalism and Society
 By Stephen B. Waters
 ISBN-13: 978-0-9845258-0-5 (Paperback)
  Library of Congress Control Number: 2010904051
 ISBN-13: 978-0-9845258-1-2 (Hardcover)
  Library of Congress Control Number: 2010905491

As accessible simple wisdoms empower people, character becomes easier to develop. New metaphors encourage processes kids understand, admire, and wish to emulate in a deeper way.

And none too soon. Journalism suffers from pervasive fog. Consciousness slips away. Schools lose traction. Character develops by chance. Politicians play games. Economists forget what works. History and philosophy drift. Scholarship loses perspective. Religion and tradition stall at cultural boundaries. Misbehavior threatens society's fragile fabric. Literature and language languish as destroyers march through civil institutions in a world made more dangerous by scientific progress. Fortunately, all it takes is a change of mind.

Table of Contents

9 AM - 1890s On journalism, narratives and belief

10 AM - 1900s On art, consciousness, and society

11 AM - On schooling children

12 PM - On exploring character

1 PM - 1910s On hope and reality

2 PM - 1920s On politics and post WWI Modernism

3 PM - 1930s On economics and citizenship

4 PM - 1940s On history and philosophy after WWII

5 PM - 1950s On scholarship and moral ambiguity

6 PM - 1960s On religion and traditions

7 PM - 1970s On literature evolving

8 PM - 1980s On empires and language

9 PM - 1990s On a long march through the culture

10 PM - 2000s On rust never sleeps

11 PM - 2010s On pivot points

12 AM - On the dawn of a new day

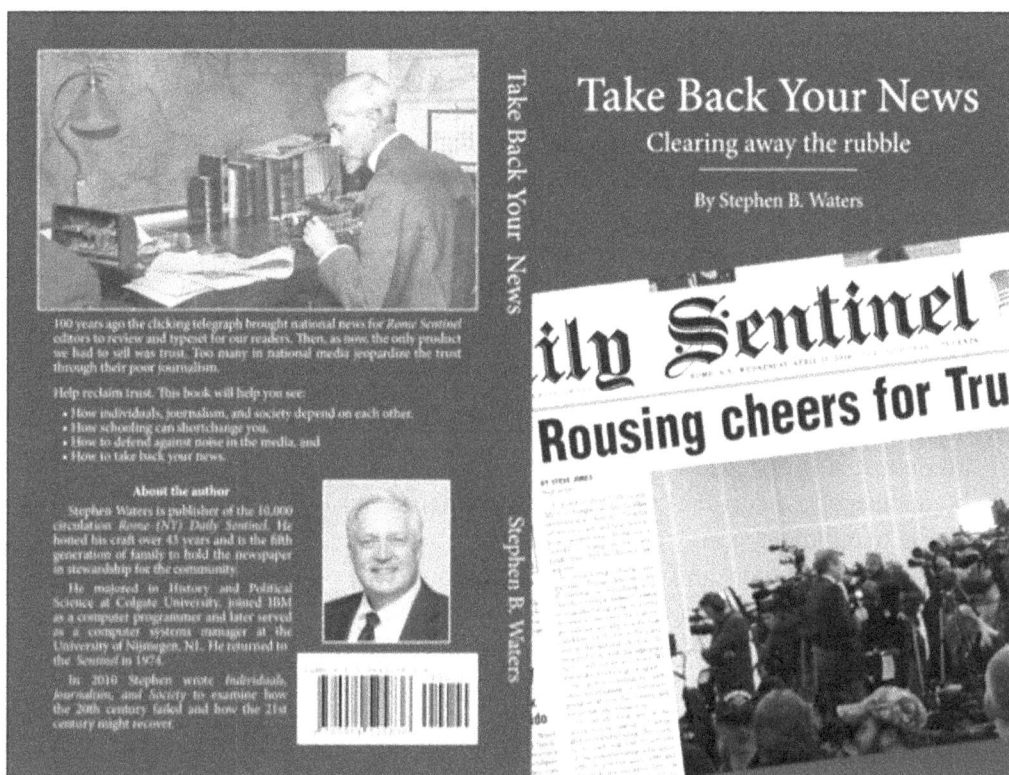

Take Back your News

By Stephen B. Waters
ISBN-13: 978-0-9845258-3-6 (Paperback)
ISBN-13: 978-0-9845258-4-3 (Hardcover)
Library of Congress Control Number: 2018901883

Help reclaim trust in journalism. This book will help you see:
- How individuals, journalism, and society depend on each other. • How schooling can shortchange you,
- How to defend against noise in the media, and
- How to take back your news.

Table of Contents

Media labels push a political agenda
Media descriptives and logical fallacies color reporting
Media manufacture messages
Media plant Improvised Editorial Devices (IEDs)
Media confuse readers with jargon
Media postmodernize word meanings

Evidence: Media sell opinion as news
Media equivocate to register opinion
Media push emotional opinion
Media speculate, project and guess
Media push unsubstantiated accusations
Media let personal views interfere

Evidence: Media accentuate narratives
Media focus their lens to affect stories
Media maps lose accuracy when details are massaged
Media manipulate context
Media compress past and present to warp context
Media preconceived narratives replace news
Media push Agitprop as news
Media fact-starved "fact-checking" isn't news

Evidence: Media obscure news
Media substitute Information for news
Media use headlines to obscure
Media misidentify content to avoid reporting
Media engage in willful ignorance
Media omit real news
Media misdirect readers
Media misdirect with innuendo
Media warp with selectively reporting
Media selectively misquote
Media breaking news is often theater
Media proffer noise as news
Media replace news with noise

Book 2: How schools fail journalism
1. Social Studies: To whom does an education belong?
2. Social Studies: To educate or to school?
3. Social Studies: A culture war
4. Social Studies: Key understandings go beyond culture
5. Social Studies: unencumbered with principles
6. Social Studies: Irrelevant themes
7. Social Studies: Specifications that misdirect
8. Social Studies: Practices that obscure history
9. Social Studies: The battle for individuals in society
10. Social Studies: Social transformation is not education
Social Studies: In summary, bring on laughter

Book 3: Where news fits in society
The Fabric of Society

A journalism to embrace
Appendices

www.ingramcontent.com/pod-product-compliance
Lightning Source LLC
Chambersburg PA
CBHW081243020426

42331CB00013B/3286